Designing America

Sean Price

Raintree

Chicago, Illinois

Customer Service: **888-454-2279**

Visit our website at **www.raintreelibrary.com**

Designed by Kimberly R. Miracle and Betsy Wernert
Photo Research by Tracy Cummins
Printed and bound in China by Leo Paper Group

12 11 10 09 08
10 9 8 7 6 5 4 3 2 1

Library of Congress Cataloging-in-Publication Data
Price, Sean.
  Designing America : the Constitutional Convention / Sean Price.
    p. cm. -- (American history through primary sources)
  Includes bibliographical references and index.
  ISBN-13: 978-1-4109-2693-7 (hardcover)
  ISBN-13: 978-1-4109-2704-0 (pbk.)
  1. United States--Politics and government--1783-1789--Juvenile literature. 2. United States. Constitutional Convention (1787)--Juvenile literature. 3. United States. Constitution--Juvenile literature. 4. Constitutional history--United States--Juvenile literature. I. Title. II. Title: Constitutional Convention.
  E303.P9 2008
  973.3--dc22

                              2007005908

Acknowledgments
The author and publisher are grateful to the following for permission to reproduce copyright material: Library of Congress Map Division **p. 4 top**; Art Resource, NY **p. 4 bottom**; U.S. National Archives **pp. 6, 24-25**; Hulton Archive/Getty Images **p. 7**; Library of Congress Prints and Photographs Division **pp. 8, 17, 19, 22–23, 27**; Library of Congress Manuscript Division **pp. 9, 20**; CORBIS **p. 11** (Francis G. Mayer), **12** (Royalty free), **13** (Bob Krist); Bettmann/CORBIS **pp. 14–15, 16, 26**; Joseph Sohm; ChromoSohm Inc./CORBIS **p. 18**; Getty Images **pp. 28** (Alex Wong), **29** (Walter Bibikow).

Cover image of *The Signing of the Constitution*, by Howard Chandler Christy (1873-1952), reproduced with the permission of Art Resource, NY.

The publishers would like to thank Nancy Harris for her assistance in the preparation of this book.

Contents

Some words are printed in bold, **like this**. You can find out what they mean on page 30. You can also look in the box at the bottom of the page where they first appear.

In the 1780s, the United States had thirteen states. ↓

↑ The Constitutional Convention was held at Independence Hall.

Constitution	most important set of laws for a country
Declaration of Independence	explains why the U.S. wanted to break away from Great Britain
Articles of Confederation	first system of laws written to unite the thirteen states

A Free Country

The U.S. **Constitution** is the most important set of rules for Americans. It is often called "the law of the land." Read this timeline. It explains why the Constitution was written.

1775 Great Britain ruled America. The British gave Americans little say in their own government. A government makes laws and runs the country. America wanted to be free from Britain. So they started the Revolutionary War. It was a war to gain freedom.

1776 Thomas Jefferson wrote the **Declaration of Independence**. This paper explained why Americans wanted to be free from Great Britain.

1781 The first thirteen states had no central government. They needed one. The states wrote the **Articles of Confederation**. It was a set of laws. The Articles created a weak central government. It could not make each state obey the laws.

1783 Americans won the Revolutionary War. They were now free from British rule.

1787 The Articles made the U.S. government too weak. U.S. leaders agreed to replace the Articles. They wrote new laws. These new laws became the U.S. Constitution.

Shays' Rebellion

The **Articles of Confederation** were written before the U.S. **Constitution**. The Articles created a weak central government. Under the Articles, U.S. leaders could make laws. But leaders had little power to make people obey laws. The government also had little money. U.S. leaders could not make people pay **taxes**. Taxes are fees that are paid to the government. The U.S. government could not even print money. Each state had its own money.

The Articles of Confederation did not make the U.S. government strong enough.

taxes	fees paid to the government
rebellion	attack upon the government
debts	money owed to others

The government's weakness showed during Shays' **Rebellion**. A rebellion is an attack on the government. In 1786, farmers from the state of Massachusetts became angry. They needed help to pay **debts**. Debts are money owed to others. Their state government would not help them. So the farmers rebelled. They were led by Daniel Shays. He was a farmer, too. The U.S. government could not stop the rebellion. U.S. leaders were too weak. Massachusetts finally created an army. That stopped the fighting. The government later forgave Shays and the other men.

Fights broke out during Shays' Rebellion.

Pushing for Change

Shays' **Rebellion** upset many people. One of them was James Madison. He was from Virginia. Madison believed the **Articles of Confederation** had to be replaced.

James Madison is often called "the father of the Constitution."

convention   large meeting

Madison had a tough job. Many Americans did not want a strong U.S. government. In the 1700s, states were more important than they are today.

People might have called themselves Americans. But more often they said, "I'm a Virginian." Or they said, "I'm a New Yorker." Many people saw each state as a separate country.

Madison kept notes during the Constitutional Convention.

Madison talked to important people. He asked them to meet. Many leaders finally agreed. Their meeting was called the Constitutional **Convention**. A convention is another word for meeting. The goal of this meeting was to create a strong central government.

The Convention was held in Philadelphia in 1787. Madison took notes during it. Most of what we know about the Convention comes from these notes. Madison is called "the Father of the Constitution."

George Washington

Americans looked up to George Washington. He had led the fight against Great Britain. His army won the Revolutionary War. America was free from British rule.

But Washington did not want to go to the Constitutional **Convention**. He liked his home in Mount Vernon, Virginia. He had also been sick. Traveling might hurt his health. There was another concern. Washington feared that the Convention would fail. He might be blamed for any failure.

But Washington was also angry about Shays' **Rebellion**. He was angry that there was an attack on the government. He wanted a stronger U.S. government. Washington decided to attend the Convention. He was named the Convention's **president**, or leader. That means he ran all the meetings.

Watching Washington

The Convention was held in Philadelphia. Meetings took place at the State House. (Later, it was called Independence Hall.) Washington walked one block to the State House each day. He was very famous. So crowds gathered to watch him. One man said Washington always "seemed pressed down in thought."

president   leader

The Convention Begins

The Constitutional **Convention** (meeting) began on May 25, 1787. Many rainstorms hit Philadelphia that summer. It was like "living under Niagara Falls," one man said. The air became hot and sticky. People dressed differently back then. Women wore long dresses, even in summer. Men wore long sleeves and jackets.

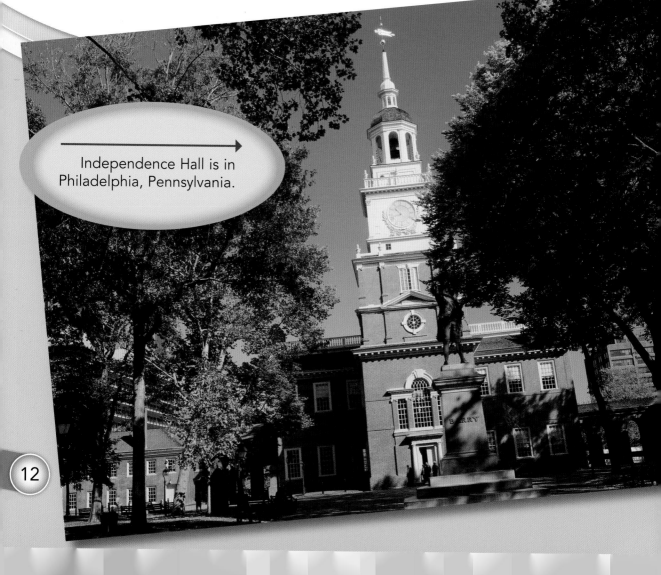

Independence Hall is in Philadelphia, Pennsylvania.

Who showed up?

Twelve of the thirteen states sent delegates. Only Rhode Island refused to send someone. Many in Rhode Island feared a strong government. They thought it would take away their rights, or freedoms.

Delegates sat in this room during the Constitutional Convention.

Fifty-five **delegates** showed up at the convention. A delegate represents someone else. These delegates spoke for the states (see map on page 4). The delegates found Philadelphia's State House hot. But they did not open the windows or doors. They put a guard at the door. The delegates did not want people to hear them. They feared people would become angry. The delegates agreed to finish the **Constitution**. Only then would they show it to other people.

Delegates argued
about how to write
the Constitution. ↑

Congress group of people who make laws for the United States
population number of people living in a place
compromise type of deal in which both sides must give up something

Settling arguments

Angry arguments almost caused the **convention** to fail many times. **Delegates** represented their states. Delegates from big states disagreed with those from small states. They disagreed over **Congress**. Congress is the group of people who make laws.

Each state was supposed to get votes in Congress. But big states said the number of votes should be based on **population**. That is the number of people living in a state. Small states did not think this was fair. They said big states could hold more people.

The two sides **compromised**. A compromise is a deal. Both sides must give up something. Big states and small states agreed to divide Congress. One part would be the Senate. The other would be the House of Representatives. Small states liked the Senate. It gave two votes to each state, no matter how big. Big states liked the House. It gave each state votes based on population. The Senate and House must agree on new laws.

A New Government

The **Articles of Confederation** made the government too weak. But **delegates** were afraid of going too far the other way. The people representing the states feared that one person might take over the government. He might become king. So the delegates broke the government into three parts, or branches.

People in the new United States tore down statues of the king of England.

Slavery and the Constitution

Delegates argued a lot about **slavery**. Slaves were black Africans. They were owned by white Americans. People in southern states liked slavery. But many from northern states thought slavery was wrong. Finally, the two sides **compromised**. Slavery was allowed to continue. But southerners agreed to stop bringing in slaves from Africa by 1808.

Congress (or **Legislative Branch**) – Makes laws

President (**Executive Branch**) – Makes sure laws are carried out

Supreme Court (**Judicial Branch**) – Makes sure laws follow the **Constitution**

Each branch is strong. But no branch is strong enough to easily take over the others. This is called "separation of powers."

A rising sun

The **Constitution** was finished. It was the most important set of laws for America. On September 17, 1787, **delegates** were asked to sign it. The delegates represented the states. Signing meant that they supported it. Each delegate disliked some part of the new Constitution. But Benjamin Franklin said, "I agree to this Constitution with all its faults." Thirty-nine of the fifty-five delegates signed.

Franklin had noticed an image on the back of George Washington's chair. The picture showed a blazing sun. Franklin wondered if it showed a setting sun. He wondered that each time the **convention** almost failed. But after the signing, Franklin said, "I have the happiness to know it is a rising, and not a setting sun."

This is the back of Washington's chair. Is the sun rising or setting? ↓

Benjamin Franklin helped make the convention a success.

Meet the delegates

Convention delegates held many different jobs. There were lawyers and bankers. There were farmers and store owners. The youngest was Jonathan Dayton. He was from New Jersey. He was 26. The oldest was Benjamin Franklin. He was from Pennsylvania. He was 81.

THE

FEDERALIST:

A COLLECTION OF

E S S A Y S,

WRITTEN IN FAVOUR OF THE

NEW CONSTITUTION,

AS AGREED UPON BY THE

FEDERAL CONVENTION,

SEPTEMBER 17, 1787.

IN TWO VOLUMES.
VOL. I.

debate	discussion between people who disagree
Federalists	supporters of the Constitution
anti-Federalists	people against the Constitution

Signing the **Constitution** was just the first step. People in the states had to vote yes or no on it. Three-quarters of the states had to vote in favor of it. That meant nine out of the thirteen states had to vote in favor of it. Otherwise, it could not become the law of the land.

This set off a heated **debate**. A debate is a discussion between people who disagree. Those in favor of the Constitution were called **Federalists**. Those who were against the new set of laws were called **anti-Federalists**. Much of their debate was carried out in newspapers.

James Madison made strong arguments for the Federalists. He wrote articles called "The Federalist." He had help from Alexander Hamilton and John Jay. Like Madison, they had pushed hard for the new Constitution. "The Federalist" articles are still read today. They are read by people who study the Constitution.

James Madison's Federalist articles are still read today.

A close race

The **anti-Federalists** were against the **Constitution**. They did not give up easily. They argued that the Constitution did not spell out people's freedoms. They also said the new set of laws created too much government power. Anti-Federalists feared that another war might be needed. A war fought to free the states from the new government!

States handled their votes on the Constitution differently. Some had state leaders vote on it. Others held an election of all the people. Massachusetts took a vote of its leaders. Like many states, the vote was close. The Constitution won by 187 votes to 168. But in Rhode Island, most voters rejected the Constitution. There were ten "No" votes to every "Yes" vote.

Finally, in June 1788, New Hampshire approved the Constitution. New Hampshire was the ninth state to approve the Constitution. That meant the Constitution became the law of the land. After that, the final four states approved it as well. Even Rhode Island finally accepted the Constitution.

This cartoon shows Federalists and anti-Federalists pulling a stuck wagon. They are pulling in different directions.

Big Changes

The **Constitution** was approved. But **Federalists** had to make a promise to get support for it. Most people felt the Constitution needed a **Bill of Rights**. This would list the things the people were free to do. The Bill of Rights became the first ten **amendments** (changes) to the Constitution. The Bill explains some of our many freedoms. They include the following:

- Freedom to speak and write

- Freedom to meet with others

- Freedom to pick a religion

- The right to a fair trial, or court case.

Making amendments

The Constitution can be amended or changed in several ways. But all of them are hard. Many states must approve of each amendment. If they don't, the amendment cannot be added to the Constitution. Delegates to the Constitutional Convention wanted it that way. They thought that amendments should be hard to pass. Each amendment should be thought out carefully.

The Constitution needed changes right away.

A success story

In 1789, George Washington stood on the balcony of New York City's Federal Hall. He was sworn in as the first U.S. **president** (leader). Like all presidents, Washington took an **oath** (pledge). In the last sentence of the oath, each president says he or she will "preserve, protect, and defend the **Constitution** of the United States."

President Washington takes an oath to protect the Constitution. Presidents still take this oath.

People admired George Washington for leading the country.

WASHINGTON'S RECEPTION BY THE LADIES, ON PASSING THE BRIDGE AT TRENTON, N.J. APRIL 1789, ON HIS WAY TO NEW YORK TO BE INAUGURATED FIRST PRESIDENT OF THE UNITED STATES.

The Constitution is our most important set of laws. It has been a huge success. But the Constitution has faced big challenges. One of the biggest was over **slavery** (owning people). The Constitution did not solve this issue. Slavery would only end after the U.S. **Civil War**. A civil war is a war between people in the same country. The U.S. Civil War lasted from 1861 until 1865. After the war, new **amendments**, or changes, were added. These ended slavery. They also gave rights to African Americans. But that is one of the strengths of the Constitution. It is **flexible**. That means it can change with the times.

Seeing the Constitution today

The U.S. **Constitution** was first written on four large pieces of paper. All four pages can be seen today in Washington, D.C. They are kept in the National **Archives**. (An archive is a kind of library.) The Constitution is displayed in a special room. The **Bill of Rights** is also there. So is the **Declaration of Independence**.

Our nation's storeroom

The National Archives holds many national treasures. It contains billions of documents, photographs, and recordings. They all show how the United States has grown since the Constitution was written.

The Constitution can be found at the National Archives in Washington, D.C.

People line up to see the Constitution and other important papers.

Each year, thousands of people come to see these **documents**. Documents are important written or printed papers. People get a special feeling at the National Archives. They see the signatures of people like Washington, Franklin, and Madison. It feels as if history has come alive. Documents like the Constitution can be seen every day. The National Archives is closed only on Thanksgiving and Christmas.

Glossary

amendment change or addition

anti-Federalists people against the Constitution

archive kind of library

Articles of Confederation first system of laws written to unite the thirteen states.

civil war war between people in the same country. The U.S. Civil War lasted from 1861–1864.

compromise type of deal in which both sides must give up something

Congress group of people who make laws for the United States

constitution most important set of laws for a country

convention gathering of people

debate discussion between people who disagree

Declaration of Independence explains why the U.S. wanted to break away from Great Britain

debts money owed to others

delegate someone who can act in the place of other people

document important written or printed paper

Federalists supporters of the Constitution

flexible can change with the times

oath pledge

population number of people living in a place

president leader of the country

rebellion attack upon the government

slaves people owned by others

taxes fees paid to the government

Want to Know More?

Books to read

- Editors of *Time for Kids*. *Benjamin Franklin: A Man of Many Talents*. New York: HarperTrophy, 2005.
- Sobel, Syl. *The U.S. Constitution and You*. Hauppauge, NY: Barron's Educational, 2001.
- Travis, Cathy. *Constitution Translated for Kids*. Austin: Synergy, 2006.

Websites

- http://www.archives.gov/national-archives-experience/charters/constitution.html *Visit this National Archives website to find out more about the Constitution's history.*
- http://www.constitutioncenter.org/explore/ForKids/index.shtml *The National Constitution Center in Philadelphia helps bring the Constitution alive.*

Places to visit

- **Independence Hall**
  Independence National Historic Park,
  143 S. Third Street, Philadelphia, PA 19106 (215) 965-2305
  Visit the rooms where the founders wrote the Constitution.

- **National Archives and Records Administration**
  700 Pennsylvania Avenue, NW, Washington, D.C. 20408-0001 (866) 272-6272
  Go and see the original Constitution and Bill of Rights.

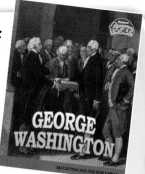

Read **George Washington: Revolution and the New Nation** to learn more about our nation's first president.

Read **A Life Well Lived: Ben Franklin** to learn about the many achievements of this founding father.

Index